brac
6/05

MAY - 2005

ALSO BY MARJANE SATRAPI

Persepolis: The Story of a Childhood
Persepolis 2: The Story of a Return

EMBROIDERIES

Embroideries

MARJANE SATRAPI

PANTHEON BOOKS, NEW YORK

L'Assoc\<ation

Pantheon Books and colophon are registered
trademarks of Random House, Inc.

Library of Congress Cataloging-in-Publication Data
Satrapi, Marjane, [date]
Embroideries / Marjane Satrapi.
    p. cm.
ISBN 0-375-42305-2
I. Title.
PN6747.S245E42 2005   741.5'944—dc22   2004058660

www.pantheonbooks.com
Printed in the United States of America
First American Edition
2 4 6 8 9 7 5 3 1

EMBROIDERIES

My grandmother called my grandfather Satrapi, never by his first name. She said one must respect one's husband.

After lunch, the men left as usual to take a nap, and the rest of us, the women, started to clean up.

Marji, my child, take care of the samovar.

Yes, Grandma.

The samovar was my responsibility. I took care of it morning, noon and night. It must be said that the morning samovar didn't play exactly the same role as at other times of the day.

The morning samovar

Grandma, do you want a cup of tea?

Shut up!

My grandma was an opium addict. The doctor had told her to take it to lessen her pain (in any case, that's what she said). And so, on waking up and finding herself in a state of withdrawal, she was often in a very very bad mood, but it never lasted for long. She had only to dissolve a small bit of burnt opium* in her tea to regain her sense of humor and her natural kindness. It was just a matter of waiting.

---

* what is left at the bottom of an opium pipe after it's been smoked.

"Opium has many virtues," my grandmother would say. "It's not just good for reducing pain."

Look at me, I have always had wide open eyes like you...

... So when I was younger, I took a little taste before going to parties. It made my eyelids heavy. It gave me a languorous look.

By the way, you should learn to close your eyes a little.

You really think that I look vibrant and intelligent like this?

No, but you'll find lovers more easily.

Thanks to her half-closed eyes, my grandma got married three times. My grandfather was her last husband.

The noon and night samovar

The tea that we prepared at these times had a completely different function.

Everyone gathered around this drink in order to devote themselves to their favorite activity: DISCUSSION.

This discussion had its own purpose:

To speak behind others' backs is the ventilator of the heart.

You must allow around three quarters of an hour for the tea to cook and reach its proper strength in a Samovar. (It really is about cooking and not steeping.)

When I finally arrived in the living room with my tray, the others had just finished the dishes.

Ah, finally!
Bravo, Marji!
May God keep you!

What timing!
Bravo, my granddaughter! Bravo!
Happiness!   Oh!   Ah!

and in this way
we began a long
session of ventilation
of the heart...

Oh, unhappy woman! If you knew how sad her life was...

Oh really? But she seemed completely fulfilled by her husband!

Yes, yes, it's true. But if you knew how sad her life was...

So tell us, Mom, instead of beating around the bush!

Well, since you insist... When she and I were young, we must have been barely 18, her parents chose a husband for her. Obviously, at the time, everyone got married that way.

The problem was that she loved another, whose name I didn't know...

...Three weeks before her wedding, I had gone out to buy something or other, when I suddenly ran into her.

 " Oooh...

 Nahid? What's the matter? Has someone died?

My life is over!

 No, no, you'll see. You'll have soon forgotten the other...

 ...In time you'll learn to love your husband.

I've lost my virginity!

 What? What do you mean? Who took it?

Gholii

 So that's what he's called, your secret lover? Why did he do that to you, that bastard?

I love him, he loves me...I had gone to say good-bye...We didn't mean to...It just happened...

Just happened!!!

Yes... I'm going to be married in 19 days. My husband will know that I'm no longer a virgin. Everyone will know! My father will kill me! Help me, I beg you, do something!!

Here, take this
little razor blade.
The night of the
honeymoon, you
squeeze your thighs
tightly, you cry out
very, very loudly and,
when the time comes,
you cut yourself a
little, but just a
very little bit!
There will be a
few drops of blood.
He'll be proud of his
virility, and you'll
keep your honor
intact.

Then came this famous night when, in the wedding chamber, she finally found herself tête-à-tête with her husband, the one whom you all knew...

So she squeezed her thighs hard...

... the gentleman hadn't even undressed, when she started to scream...

You're right. It's true that I had four kids. Four!! But I still have never seen the male organ. He came into the bedroom, he turned off the light...

... And then,
Bam !
    Bam !
        Bam !

And voilà, I was pregnant! What's more, I was granted four girls. So I've never seen penises!

At the time, I had
thick eyebrows that
met in the middle.
Like this!

It was torture to have
them pulled out one by
one. They cut my hair
and my mother had a
dress made on which
she had some 1,200
pearls stitched.
Then, they made me
up, perfumed me...
all so that I would
please an old man!

... In the end, I looked like a little whore ...

... I was married as planned. A few hours later, I found myself shut up in the house of the old guy ...

... I took one look at his wrinkled back and realized that it wasn't possible. So I made my decision.

... My aunt had much more modern ideas than my parents. And she was a widow, which allowed her to think and to act for herself. So she took me in.

My father, my mother and my brothers tried everything to get me to return to my dear and tender husband. I said, "No!".

But the worst was yet to come. The old guy didn't want a divorce!

I made a thousand prayers for him to die.

It's not disgusting, that little skin that hangs?

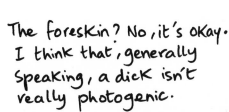

The foreskin? No, it's okay. I think that, generally speaking, a dick isn't really photogenic.

I quite agree.

Us? Well, if you'd like, we could get married. Then, nothing will ever be able to separate us. I'll leave first and you will join me in Berlin a few months from now. Do you want to? Would you like to become my wife?

Imbecile! What a question. It's my greatest dream!!!

My father accepted his request right away because the whole city knew about Houshang and me. The quicker I got married, the quicker my family would regain its lost honor... Finally... December 19, 1953, was the most beautiful day of my life. We had organized a little party... family and some close friends. There were 60 or 70 of us altogether.*

Look! I still carry a photo of this day with me. I've never been separated from it for 38 years...

* In Iran, if one has the means, one must invite at least 300 people.

... See how happy my parents look!

... He didn't inspire my confidence. Anyway, I never saw him again. He scared me. When we finally arrived ...

In my whole life, I'd never seen such a dilapidated place! I had to wait five more hours before my so-called husband came home...

Oh, my darling, my beautiful one, my sweet, Oh, I missed you so much! Oh, Oh!

...He smelled like woman. He explained that he hadn't had the time to furnish our "Love nest." I asked him what his work was. He answered that he devoted all his time to his political activities... He was undoubtedly busy with the diplomatic relations between his testicles and women's breasts!

All that he'd learned of western culture was to slick back his hair more and to kiss on the right and the left...

... After the second week, he started coming home later and later. Every night I would wait for him at the window, and every night I saw him get out of a taxi with a new woman ... He kissed them in a way he'd never kissed me!

When I asked him who these women were, he told me that they were comrades, that it was politics, that he preferred that I stay out of all that!

And I wanted so much to believe him that I let myself be taken for a fool!

I lasted a year all the same, but the situation couldn't continue. I was on the verge of going crazy.

So I decided to fill my days. I registered to learn German at the Goethe Institute in the mornings, and in the evenings I took a dance class. That's where I met Herbert. He was my waltz partner.

I sensed that he wanted to seduce me, but I was a married woman, so I couldn't give in to him. The more I saw Herbert, the less I could stand my life with Houshang! I finally let myself go. Herbert was so charming. No one had ever satisfied me like him. Just one kiss and I was already in seventh heaven...

Oh my, oh my! What stupidity, really, what stupidity...

...to be the mistress of a married man is to have the better role...

... After my trip to Europe, I became the lover of a minister...

... It was perfect ...

.. Do you realize?

His dirty shirts,

His disgusting underwear,

His daily ironing,

His bad breath,

His hemorrhoid attacks,

Aiii!

His flus,

Help me...

Not to mention his bad moods...

...and his tantrums...

I don't like eggplant!

... Well, all that is for his wife.

... He is there to have a good time with you.

Come on, tell!

Don't be high and mighty, my child!

Go ahead! We're listening!!

Go on, go on!!

I love stories!

Look, I also told my story!

I beg you, tell!!

Please...

NO!

I see that
trust rules...

Listen to me. I'm
your mother. Tell !

We won't tell
anyone...

Do it for
Grandma!

Don't feel
pressured !

Stories are
very good !

Yes ...

Please,
Please !

Pfff ...

Do you all know Shideh?

The breadboard with a horse face?

That's her! Well, she got married at 17 to the first guy who came along to get away from her parents, who tyrannized her. Two years later, after her sexual needs had been satisfied, she realized that she had nothing in common with this man. It was hell for her to get her divorce. I had stopped seeing her during this whole period because I hated her husband. I thought him an absolute zero. I ran into her by chance last year at a party. She had changed a lot...

It's you, Shideh! I didn't recognize you. The last time I saw you, you were a brunette!

Yes, I have decided to take my life into my own hands. I want to find a man who understands and respects me. Your prayers work. Say one for me.

The other day she called to ask me if I wanted to accompany her to see a woman who does white magic.

White magic? Ha, ha, ha ...

... Oh yeah? You're really serious?

Okay. We'll meet at your house at five o'clock. I'll come get you.

There, take a right!

We arrived at a seedy alley. I didn't even know that these kinds of streets existed in Tehran.

I think it's there!

Here! Take this key. You prepare some tea.
You sleep with him. Once he's ejaculated—
careful!— he must come in you—you put the
key in your vagina. You count to 7.
Then you remove the key and put
it into a cup. You pour the tea
on top. You count to 7. The
last step is to remove the
key. Tea prepared like this
should be drunk by your heart's
chosen one in the 77 seconds that follow
ejaculation. There, that'll be 3,000 tumans.*

* equivalent to $40 in 1991 (thanks to inflation)

Yes, ladies!
I had my fat
removed from here.

...And I had it
injected here.

At present, my breasts are
my husband's sole object
of attention.
He can't stop telling me
that I'm beautiful and
desirable, that I look
like Brigitte Bardot, that
I'm the best thing that ever
happened to him in his
life, that this, that
that...

You always thought that...
What? That this little pointed
thing was my natural nose?
Frankly, do you know one
single person in the family who
has this nose?

... No, my dear!
I had inherited
the majestic
nose of my late
father. Mine
was almost a
perfect copy of his.
Those who knew
him recognized me
and vice versa.

My nose was so enormous that if someone sat
on my right, it was impossible for him to see what
was happening on my left.

So I told myself since your nose is super-ugly, I could redo it for you.

!

And you're the one who will perform the operation?

Oh no! It will be a plastic surgeon...

...

...And also don't worry about the money. I've spoken to Payman about it. We're going to find a solution.

Ah! Because Payman also thinks that my nose is "super-ugly"?

Of course! Everyone thinks so.

Their solution consisted of buying biscuits and cigarettes at the supermarket and reselling them a little more expensively in the street. Taji played the role of the supplier.

 I had no choice, Mom! You know as well as I do that they were so motivated it would have been difficult to do otherwise. They spent one whole summer sitting behind a cardboard box that served as a counter to earn some cash.

 My mom is right. We worked like dogs, but we loved Grandma so much that we were capable of any sacrifice, provided that she would have a beautiful nose in the end.

How much is it?

Six tumans, please.

But next-door it's four tumans.

Yes, we know, but we need money.

For what?

It's a secret.

In that case, give me two more packs!

Since we were little, we quite easily charmed our neighbors, who bought lots of cigarettes and biscuits from us. We deposited all the earnings in a piggy bank. By the end of the summer we had collected 750 tumans, but what we needed was 7,500 tumans.

So what did you do?

To get them to forget their disappointment in not having enough money for their grandmother's operation, I took them to a toy store where they blew all of it in less than five seconds.

And so my child, since you preferred your toys to my nose, I'm offering you a chance to redeem yourself. Make me a gift of a full embroidery.

HA! HA!
HA! HA!
HA! HA!
HA! HA!
HA! HA!
HA! HA!
HA!

Listen! I have had two children like you. I think a vagina is like a rubber band. There are good quality rubber bands that stay elastic, even when you pull on them 150 times, and there are others that stretch out after two uses.

If you had only seen the face on the woman who wanted to be taken in! I was dying of laughter! So you see, you can do the same!

No! For me, it's all or nothing...

...to think that if this poor Nahid had been born in this epoch, she would have been able to have herself embroidered instead of cutting her poor husband!

Don't forget that you're the one who advised her to do it!

As far as I know, I have never encouraged anyone to cut balls.

Can you explain to me why a man of 41 who has lived in Europe practically his whole life and who is educated wants to marry a girl of 18?

Well, you know how western girls are... They're no longer pure, starting at ages ten, eleven. He's an Iranian. He has certain values, and it's all to his credit!

Listen, Parvaneh! Since you came to see me, I suppose that I have the right to give my opinion: Look, I think that you are on your way to making a big mistake! Bahar is very young. Let her study, be independent, become someone! You yourself married the man of your choice. Give her the opportunity and the time to grow up and decide for herself.

And the result? Every time I fight with "the man of my choice," he reproaches me for having run after him, meaning that a good girl would have waited for him to ask for her hand.

No, Taji! She will be married. She'll still have the advantage of her youth, unlike me who gets called "old bag" all the time!

I tried in vain to explain to my idiot of a cousin that one doesn't send one's child into the arms of a stranger with the excuse that he's rich, that money isn't everything in life... but there was nothing to be done. She'd made her decision! Finally came the night of the wedding...

... The whole way there, from my house to the celebration, I couldn't stop myself thinking of this poor child.

But a picture of her husband !!!

I went to find Ebi, and we went home right away. If I had stayed, I would undoubtedly have put my fist in her mouth.

Finally... a week later Bahar left for London to rejoin her husband, and two months after her departure, Parvaneh came to see me again...

Oh dear, Taji! She fled her husband's house! Oh dear!... She told me that every night instead of sleeping in the bed, well, her husband slept under the bed. Under the bed! Can you imagine ???... He slept under the bed and let out cries like a jackal.

Aouuuu... Aouuu...

What's this?

So her husband is something of a psychopath. Just because one plays a jackal under the bed does not mean that one is a homosexual.

Yes...only...he has everything wrong with him. He is a psychopath and gay...

Oh, Taji! Bahar told me all kinds of terrible stories... One day she came home from the supermarket, and there was apparently another man in their house who put his hand on her husband's thigh. Another time she surprised him and this time it was he who had his hands on the thigh of another man. Another time, she saw him kiss three guys at the same time...

... but okay, in every misfortune, there is always something positive. My daughter is still a virgin. She has every chance of remarrying.

God, make her shut up!!!

Azzi was our neighbor.

She had moved into our building two years before. She lived with her sister and her parents. She was very kind and very discreet. So discreet that no one knew anything about her life.

... year of studying to be a nurse. One day, when I got back from school, my mother told me that one of our neighbors had come to see her to ask for my hand for her nephew, who lived in Switzerland and who was looking to marry a good Iranian girl from a good family.

My parents told me that the decision was entirely up to me. I thought about it for a long time. I also talked about it a lot with my sister and my girlfriends.

If I were in your place, I'd be wary.

In your place, I wouldn't hesitate for a single second. You have the chance to live in Europe, to not wear the veil anymore! To be free!!! ... What more could you want?

Here, in Iran, we have no future. Go ahead, get married, leave!!

I took my sister's wariness for jealousy...
Also I wanted so much to leave for the west.
Every time I watched MTV, I told myself that life was elsewhere.

What's MTV?

You know, it's that music channel!

The one with all the assholes who sing half naked?

Yes, Grandma!

Oh, this poor Azzi is so stupid!

Finally, after thinking about it a thousand times, I told my parents that it was okay with me. So my mother called the neighbor, who right away called her brother and sister-in-law, so that they would come and officially ask for my hand. They brought me this photo of him, saying that he would be in Tehran in a month, because even if their son was handsome and intelligent and nice, I should get to know him before getting engaged! Look, this is him!

In short, he agreed with everything I said. If you knew the promises he made me! For example, he told me that I could continue my studies if I wanted since he already had a maid who took care of all the cleaning.

Anyone in my place would have fallen for his pretty words.

... And so we were married. I went to the best hairdresser in Tehran. Ever since my dear and earliest childhood, I had wished for only one thing, and that was to see myself dressed as a bride. My dream had just come true. Even better, my dress was made by Mrs. Tabatabai, you know, the super-famous designer. We received 700 guests. I was offered so many jewels I would have needed several more fingers, arms, ears and necks to be able to wear them all. It was incredible. *

* During a wedding in Iran, almost all the gifts are for the bride.

So! He left with my jewelry. I didn't hear any news from him for two months. I tried to convince myself that he was too busy with his hotels and his society events. Finally one day...

Azzi! You have a letter!

A letter? From whom?

From your husband!

God be praised!

So, so! What does he say? Is it done? Is your visa ready?

Sh, Oh

He... He wants a divorce

Boohoohoo...he divorced me ...
boohoo...he spent one night with
me and he divorced me!...

Just one night and I lost
everything! Boohoo ... everything!
My virginity, my jewels...

That you're crying for your jewels, I
understand. It's not every day that
you're given gifts of many Kilos of gold.
But as far as your virginity is concerned...
Now that you are married and divorced,
it's normal that you're no Longer a
virgin! You can make Love with whomever
you want, without anyone Knowing!

You Know! There's no meter
down here!

But no one will want to
marry a girl who's divorced!!

Stop, attitudes
change even in men!

NO...

Yes! I have a cousin who always maintained that he would only marry a virgin. The other day he called me to tell me that he had changed his mind. When I congratulated him on his enlightenment, he answered: "Marji, if I changed my mind, it's because no girls are virgins anymore." That's what he told me word for word. Do you see?

That's life!
Sometimes
you're on the
horse's back,
and sometimes
it's the horse
that's on
your back.

Marjane Satrapi was born in 1969 in Rasht, Iran. She now lives in Paris, where she is a regular contributor to magazines and newspapers throughout the world, including *The New Yorker* and *The New York Times*. She is the author of several children's books, as well as a critically acclaimed and internationally best-selling memoir published in two volumes as *Persepolis: The Story of a Childhood* and *Persepolis 2: The Story of a Return*. *Persepolis* has been translated into twelve languages, was a *New York Times* Notable Book, and received the Harvey Award for best American edition of foreign material and an Alex Award from the American Library Association.